YOU CAN STOP WORRYING

JAY E. ADAMS

BAKER BOOK HOUSE
Grand Rapids, Michigan

ISBN: 0-8010-0097-1
Printed in the United States of America

Joe's friends all knew him as a worrier. One day Bill saw his worrying friend bouncing along as happy as a man could be, whistling and humming and wearing a huge smile; he looked as if he did not have a care in the world. Bill could hardly believe his eyes, so he had to find out what had happened.

"Joe, what's happened to you?" he asked. "You don't seemed worried any more." "It's wonderful, Bill, I haven't worried for several weeks now." "That's great; how did you manage it?" Joe explained, "I hired a man to do all of my worrying for me." "What?" "Right." "Well," Bill mused, "I must say that that is a new wrinkle; tell me, how much does he charge you?" "A thousand dollars a week." "A thousand dollars a week? How could you possibly raise a thousand dollars a week to pay him?" Joe answered, "That's *his* worry."

Wouldn't that be great? Don't you wish it were possible for someone else to handle your worries for you? Well, the Bible says that it is possible; indeed God encourages His children to cast all of their cares on *Him* (I Pet. 5:7). And what is best of all—that arrangement won't cost you a cent. God freely offers to take your worries and cares upon Himself. Because He does, and because He has ordered us not to worry, all worry is sin. Constantly in Scripture

God tells us not to worry. When we disobey His Word, that is sin. Worry, perhaps, is *the* American sin.

THE EFFECTS OF WORRY

Worry can put ulcers on the stomach, sap vitality out of living, and drive us to an early death. Worry makes us incapable of handling life's problems. Worry shows lack of faith in God, and keeps us from assuming responsibilities and serving Jesus Christ. Worry is sin.

Perhaps you are letting worry keep you from living as faithfully as Christ would like. Perhaps you even worry about your worry! What you want to know is, *what can be done about it?* What does the Bible have to say about overcoming this sin? It says you can overcome it; you really can.

Many Christians are stymied by this problem. Phil, an engineer, had been given the task of building a large office buildng. This assignment was larger than any he had ever handled, and it was full of problems—that he allowed to get to him. He began to worry about them. The contractors and the subcontractors were fighting; the electricians and the carpenters couldn't get along. Deadlines were not being met. He worried about the job day after day, becoming more and more immobile and less able to handle day-by-day problems. As he looked at his job day after day he concluded, "It's just too much; I can't take it." Finally one day he laid down his pencil, got up out of his chair, turned around and walked out of the room. Phil was a Christian, and came for counseling. There he found the answer.

What is worry? In the Bible the word *worry* usually is translated "anxiety," or "care." It ought to be translated "worry," so that we understand in contemporary language what God is talking about. The Greek word for worry in the New Testament means "to divide, part, rip or tear apart." The word describes the *effects* of worry; that is what worry *does* to us. But worry itself is *concern over the future*. Worry is concern about something that one *can do nothing about,* and that he *cannot even be sure about*. That is why it tears us apart. One who worries looks off into the future. But the future is not here yet. There is nothing to lay a hand on; there is nothing that can be done. The worrier cannot control it; he does not even know what it will look like. No one but God knows its true shape. First, the worrier imagines that matters will be this way, then (he thinks), they might be that way. Because he cannot know, he allows worry to tear him apart. "If that is what worry is," you say, "what can I do about it?"

Listen to Jesus; He has the answer. He says "Do not worry" (Matt. 6:31). But He does not leave the matter there; He explains how to overcome worry. He concludes a vital discussion concerning anxiety over life's necessities with these significant words: "Therefore do not be anxious about tomorrow, for tomorrow will be anxious for itself" (Matt. 6:34). Jesus made it clear that what is wrong with worry is that it is the wrong focus on life. Jesus says that it is wrong to let *tomorrow's* possible problems tear you apart *today*.

Christ contrasts two days: "Do not worry about tomorrow because tomorrow will take care of itself. . . ." "Sufficient unto the day is the trouble thereof." In these words you have God's answer to worry. Each day has enough trouble of its own. Don't focus your concern upon tomorrow's problems; there are enough problems to handle today. Tomorrow always belongs to God. Tomorrow is in His hands. Whenever we try to take hold of it, we try to steal what belongs to Him. Sinners want what is not theirs to have, and thereby destroy themselves. God has given us only today. He strongly forbids us to become concerned about what *might* happen. That is entirely in His hands. The tragic fact is that worriers not only want what has been forbidden, but also fail to use what has been given to them.

But before we go any further, one point must be made clear: Christ does not object to planning for tomorrow. He does not oppose thinking about tomorrow or preparing for tomorrow; what He forbids is worry, the sort of anxiety that tears one to shreds. There is nothing in Matthew 6 against planning for tomorrow.

James' words are crucial to an understanding of this matter (James 4:13ff.). Some have mistakenly understood James to say that he is against all kinds of planning. But that is exactly the opposite of his intention. Indeed, in that passage he explains *how* to plan. He forbids improper planning, but at the same time shows how to plan as God requires. Planning and worry are two entirely different matters.

"How should one plan?" you wonder. James answers that question: "You ought to say, *If the Lord wills,* we shall live and also do this or that. But as it is, you boast in your arrogance; all such boasting is evil." Now you see the difference. James says that you must plan (you can't avoid planning) *without worry*. Because the worrier acts as if he holds the future in the palm of his hand, he is arrogant. James says that you must lay your plans before God and say, "Lord, to the best of my ability I have tried to sketch out my plans according to your will as I have learned it in the Bible, but, Lord, you are sovereign; I submit my plans to you. Your will must be done."

As a Christian, you know that your life belongs to God by creation. But you also have been bought with a price by the death of Jesus Christ, who gave His life to redeem you from sin and eternal death. Your next breath is in His hands. So you must say, "Lord, I lay my plans before you for blue penciling." When you plan that way, submitting your plans to the Lord for revision (or scrapping), joyously accepting the scratched-over page that He may hand back to you, then you plan as James says you should. That is the only way for a Christian to look forward to tomorrow. Planning that is subject to God's alterations is planning that does not lead to worry. What is there to worry about when you truly put your best plans into God's hands?

Now then, let us return to Matthew 6 to discover Jesus' alternative to worry. What can you do about your concern if, as Jesus says, you must not be worried about tomorrow? You cannot turn off concern; it is impossible to be free from concern. "How can I turn off my emotions?" you plead. In the answer to that question lies the key to the problem of worry. Christ does not ask you to stop being concerned; instead, He tells you to *redirect your concern*. Concern ought not be focused on tomorrow; such concern tears us apart.

If you have laid your best plans in the Lord's hands, you can turn your attention away from tomorrow. You need no longer be concerned about that, but your concern, your efforts, your energies, all that you have now can be poured into *today*. That is the key that locks the door on worry and opens the door to peace: *focus your concern upon today*.

Concern is right, not wrong. Every emotion that God has put in man is right in its right place. It is right when it is properly used according to the commandments and principles of His word. But every emotion may be used wrongly. Emotional concern is the God-given ability to mobilize the forces of the body and the mind to focus on a problem. But when those forces are focused on tomorrow, the purpose of the chemical and electrical energies of the body is frustrated, because they are poured into the body, but not used. They cannot be released in action, because we cannot *act* upon the future. Worry activates more and more energy that is unused, some of which in chemical form may eat away at the lining of the stomach.

If you focus on today, then energy is not wasted, but will be used. Your concern will count; your energies can be used fruitfully in the service of Jesus Christ to *solve* problems rather than to *worry* about them. That is what Jesus is saying: "Do not be anxious for tomorrow, for tomorrow will care for itself. Each day has enough trouble of its own." Take care of today's problems; take *care* of the troubles that you have to handle now. That is the key to eliminating worry.

Concern for today's problems does not tear you up, *because* you can get a handle on them. You can do something about today's problems. You can do something because they are *here*; you are dealing with reality. Phil learned that he could do something about today's problems. First, we sat down and looked at the problems, and sketched out a tentative plan for the whole, putting it into the Lord's hands in prayer. Then we looked more closely at the coming week to determine (if the Lord wills) what Phil might do this week. Finally we looked at *to day* and asked: "What can be done right now?" Phil had been looking at the whole forest and had concluded that it was too dark, too thick, and too large to cut down. Instead, Phil had to learn to say, "By the grace of God three trees are coming down today." Then, he was to focus and concentrate all of his energy on chopping down those three trees. He must forget the rest. The next day he must take down three more, and the following day three more, and possibly the next day four. As he continued to chop them down, three or four a day, the time came when he began to see daylight on the other side of the forest. Phil solved the problem of worry by solving each day's problems one day at a time.

If you work faithfully for Christ, doing what you can about the problems that present themselves today, using all of your energies, you can go home tonight tired but satisfied. How long has it been since you have had that good feeling; not that tired-dissatisfied, but that tired-but-satisfied feeling at the end of the day that comes only when you go to bed knowing that you have expended your energies as God has directed you?

Do you know that Scripture indicates that many worrying people are *lazy*? Well, that is what Jesus Himself said about one worrier who was afraid of the future, and sought to be excused from his present responsibilities on the basis of worry. Jesus called him lazy. In

Matthew 25, Christ told the story of three servants who were given money to invest. When their lord returned, he inquired about their investments. The one who had been given the most doubled the amount, and the second did the same. But the third confessed that he hid his money in the ground. When the lord returned he dug it up, brought it to him and said, "Here is your money, lord. I buried it because I was afraid" (v. 25). The slave worried about the possible consequences of investing the money. He worried and worried, and worried, and became paralyzed. He worried and did not work. But his master answered, "You wicked (note, it is sinful to worry), lazy slave . . . You ought to have put my money in the bank, and on my arrival I would have received my money back with interest" (Matt. 25:25, 26), i.e., "At least you should have done the minimal thing you could, but you didn't. You are a lazy slave."

The worrier *can't* do anything because he is working on tomorrow's problem. But that really boils down to no work at all. You can't do anything about unknown problems that are yet in the future. Worrying is like rocking in a rocking chair; you expend a lot of energy but you don't get anywhere. *Something* can always be *done* about today's problem (cf. I Cor.

10:13). Even if you can't change a thing outside of yourself, by the sanctifying power of the Holy Spirit your attitudes toward problems can be changed. *You* can change if nothing else will. There is always something, then, that can be done.

Here is a simple procedure that you might want to use when you find yourself worrying instead of working. Instead of worrying, immediately sit down and write out the following three questions on a piece of paper, leaving spaces beneath each so that you can fill them in later.

1. What is my problem?

2. What does God want me to do about it?

3. When, where, and how should I begin?

Sometimes just defining a problem by forcing yourself to write it out leads to a solution. When the problem is defined, you must begin immediately to look for the solution in Scripture. Ask, "How can I handle this problem for the glory of God?" But then, don't settle for good solutions and noble ideals; get to work. Schedule your actions and put the hardest task first. Don't forget Abraham, who got up *early*,

Scripture says, when he was given the heart-rending command to sacrifice Isaac, his only son, whom he loved (Gen. 22:3). There you have God's solution to worry.

One final thought. This booklet is written for Christians but if it should happen that you do not know Jesus Christ as your Savior, let me say a word to you. While God says that Christians do not have anything to worry about, you have *everything* to worry about. There is no such promise as that Romans 8:28 for you. That promise was made exclusively to God's own: "all things work together for good *to those who love God.*" There is no solution but unending hell at the end of your road. The Bible pictures hell as a place of utter darkness and loneliness. Persons in hell are like wandering stars, light years away from each other! (Jude 13). Worse still, they will wander forever in isolation and darkness from the presence of God: "And these will pay the penalty of eternal destuction, away from the presence of the Lord and from the glory of His power" (II Thess. 1:9). That is the most terrible fact of all. Hell is going to be an extremely lonely place where men, instead of worrying about the future, will anguish in memory of the past. There alone is the future certain; there the terror of an everlasting future apart from God will be the awful certainty.

Perhaps God has been working in your heart to convict you of your sin. Possibly He has put this pamphlet into your hands because He wants you to put your trust in Jesus Christ. Jesus died on the cross in the place of guilty sinners like you, taking their hell for them. All who believe that He died for them are forgiven, and instead, receive the gift of eternal life—a life forever with God in heaven. God promises, "As many as received Him [Jesus Christ], to them He gave the right to be called the children of God, even to those who believe in His name" (John 1:12). Why don't you trust Him right now? Don't merely worry—act! Act in obedience to the Word of God.

To those of you who know Him, let me ask, "Do you need to repent of the sin of worry?" Do so, then take each day's problems as they come, and do business that day for Jesus Christ.